110 Ways To Champion Diversity And Build Inclusion

"This is a simple tool filled with a variety of good ideas that when implemented will certainly help set the tone for a more inclusive and rewarding workplace. Actions do speak louder than words and this booklet gives you and anyone in your organization 110 ideas to get started on."

Nadia Younes
Group Adviser, Diversity and Inclusion
Rio Tinto

"110 Ways To Champion Diversity And Build Inclusion is helpful for those who are ready to take action on D&I issues. It is concrete and specific and backed up by Simma's knowledge, practicality, and experience in achieving results."

Julie O'Mara
D&I consultant and author of Global Diversity and Inclusion Benchmarks: Standards for Organizations Around the World

"This book presents practical and creative ways to build an inclusive work culture in any organization. Simma shows us how people at any level can take actions to advance diversity and be more successful."

Mercedes Martin
EY , executive coaching team
Cross cultural coaching

D0569975

- -

"This booklet is concise, easy to read, and comprehensive. I can think of many different uses and venues where it would be value-added, especially to Diversity and Inclusion leaders who are looking for activities and initiatives to implement."

Tommy E. Smith Jr.
Pastor, Palma Ceia Baptist Church
Former Director, Office of Strategic Diversity Initiatives,
Lawrence Livermore National Laboratory

"Are you at loss as to how to energize your organization with diversity and inclusion activities? Simma makes it easy in this concise booklet; a perfect accompaniment for leadership training, diversity and inclusion practitioners and anyone who is searching for ways to make their workplaces better."

Evelina Silveira, President
Diversity At Work in London Inc.
Author Diversity and Inclusion on a Budget: How to have a more engaged and innovative workforce with little or no dollars

I would like to acknowledge the following people for helping me create this booklet; Julie O'Mara, Linda Popky, Roberta Matuson, Charmaine McClarie, Nadia Younes, Pastor Tommy Smith, Mercedes Martin, Michelle Meow and the cast of Swirl, Bonnie Lieberman and Michael Hart, Irfan Idrees, Kim Wilkerson, Scott Simmonds, Rick Pay, David Aguirre, Christine Simmonds, Evelina Silveira, Avi Lieberman, Eric Graham, and Betty Rowe.

Leveraging diversity, and creating an inclusive work culture involves much more than race and gender. It is more than what looks good in a company photo. It is knowing how to champion diversity and create a culture where everyone has the opportunity to do his best work no matter who he is, what he does, or where he works. In an inclusive workplace, everyone feels like a part of the organization and knows how she contributes to the success of the business. Diversity management and inclusion are integrated into every system and process.

While each individual action in this booklet helps the organization and the people in it move closer to inclusion, practicing only one is not enough to create sustainable change. All are necessary to leverage the diversity of your workforce.

Both managers and employees are continually asking, "What can we do, and what can I do?"

These are over a hundred actions that individual employees and managers can practice right away, as well as actions that are specific to people in leadership positions.

This booklet demonstrates that diversity is complex and includes everyone, and that training and/or programs like lunch-and-learns are not "the answer," but are pieces of the culture change process.

These actions come from hands-on work in organizations, best practices from employees and managers, and ideas suggested by people at all organizational levels. It is modeled after and inspired by the book "101 Actions You Can Take to Value and Manage Diversity" written by Julie O'Mara in 1999 who recently told me she liked my thinking and that I needed to create a new booklet.

Leveraging diversity and creating an inclusive work culture is the result of every person in the organization being actively involved in the process. The following actions and insights are universal and for everyone, regardless of title or position.

1. Learn the definition of these four terms in relationship to your workplace:

    A. **Diversity:** Roosevelt Thomas, one of the pioneers of diversity in organizations today, defined it as "the collective mixture of differences and similarities in the workplace with related tensions and complexities."

    B. **Inclusion/Inclusive culture:** A culture where everyone feels welcome, and has the opportunity to be successful and contribute fully to the organization.

    C. **Diversity Management:** "The process of creating and maintaining an environment that naturally enables all participants to contribute to their full potential in focused pursuit of organizational objectives." (Roosevelt Thomas)

    Good diversity management leverages the complexity of those similarities and differences for individual and organizational success.

- -

D. **Cultural Intelligence:** Having the capacity and knowledge to work effectively with people from any cultural group whether or not you have any prior experience.

2. Become aware of your biases and assumptions about people who are different than you.

Everyone has biases based on his or her background and what has been heard about different groups of people from families, friends, religious leaders, or the media. People make assumptions as a result of those biases.

Think about the messages you received growing up about people who were different, and the biases you formed as a result. Being conscious of our biases today, and their origin, is the first step in breaking through them.

Be conscious of your visceral reaction or any thoughts or judgments you have about the next three people you see. What are your initial thoughts? Based on your very first impression, what story would you create about them?

Bias Destruction

Notice their age, clothing, skin color, and any other visible characteristics at the root of your bias and first story.

Next, create a different story about what they do and who they are. Seeing other possibilities will help filter out your biases and wrong assumptions about people.

> **Example:** You're an extroverted White woman at a large dinner party in the middle of a discussion with people sitting near you.
>
> You're sitting next to a Black woman named Charlene who is not looking at you or engaging in your discussion. You turn your back to Charlene and ignore her the rest of the evening.

After the dinner you approach the host and tell her that you think Charlene doesn't like White people because she wouldn't talk to you.

The host, who is also White, informs you that Charlene is her best friend and is extremely introverted, doing much better in direct one-on-one interaction, and that in fact the two of you share a love of spectator sports.

Ask yourself, what made you assume that Charlene's actions had anything to do with race?

3. Check the accuracy of your assumptions before you act on them. Wrong assumptions based on personal biases can result in mistreated people, negatively affected working relationships, and can be detrimental to your organization.

4. Think before you put a label on another person based on generalizations and stereotypes. Biases and assumptions lead to stereotyping and excluding people from fully contributing to an organization.

Let go of the label

If a co-worker tells you that a new employee is arrogant, or a know-it-all, there is a tendency to assume that's the truth, and you may find yourself looking for signs that the person fits the label.

Think of someone that you labeled based on another person's comment. How did you treat that person because of that label?

When you find yourself labeling someone, instead, become curious and talk to him or her. Don't pre-judge them based on the word of someone else.

Take the time to get to know the whole person before you label him or her based on looks, accent, size, skin color, etc.

5.   View situations from more than one vantage point.

Everyone sees the world based on his or her own cultural values and personal experiences. When you interact with people who have different cultural values and experiences, you must try to imagine what the world looks like through that person's eyes.

Think of two possible interpretations of a situation or issue besides your own. You'll be able to better resolve conflicts, find common ground, and work effectively together when you are open to other points of view, even if you don't agree with them.

Put yourself in someone else's head to understand why he or she came to a certain conclusion. Listen to the person's words and imagine yourself living those experiences.

 This will help you understand why another person feels and acts a certain way. Understanding a person does not mean you agree on all issues; but you will work better with that individual. Seeing the world, workplace, and other people from someone else's perspective may change yours, change theirs, or help you determine the best way to get the results you want.

Don't just empathize with people's feelings; try to understand why. Without understanding why a coworker might be feeling a certain way, it's easy to tell her that she shouldn't feel that way, or to discount her feelings, which can result in the other person feeling excluded, and not contributing her best work.

6.   Talk with and get to know people from different generations.

Avoid blanket statements like:

- Baby boomers don't understand technology.

- They can't change.

- Young people have no work ethic.

- Facebook keeps people from interacting.

Instead, consider what you can learn from the other generations, and what they can learn from you.

Just because you may not understand another generation's music, hobbies, or interests doesn't mean they are not valid. You can ask what they like about a type of music, a specific artist, or area of interest.

With greater understanding you get a new appreciation. There are plenty of people under thirty listening to Frank Sinatra, Marvin Gaye, and The Rolling Stones, as well as people over fifty listening to Beyonce, John Legend, and even hip-hop.

7.   Try foods from different cultures, and then read about their origins, and whether they have any special meanings.

8.   Be curious and express interest in other people and cultures. Learn how to ask questions in appropriate ways about food, rituals, working with others, and what they want you to know about them.

Are you willing to take a risk, observe other people's behaviors and ask questions in appropriate ways? If you're not interested or willing to view situations from another perspective, it won't matter how many countries you visit or diversity potlucks you attend.

That can mean putting yourself in situations with people from different cultures and being willing to admit you don't know a lot about their culture but want to learn.

9. Research your own cultural background and identify ways in which your culture and early experiences have influenced your behavior. Recognize the fact that other people's behavior is influenced by their own backgrounds and experiences, which may be very different than yours.

10. Stop stereotyping whole groups and individuals from those groups.

When people are seen as stereotypes, they are no long individuals or equals.

Think of people you know personally, from those goups, such as a co-worker, neighbor, or former classmate or who are well-known and admired like Nelson Mandela. You'll be better able to filter out those group stereotypes.

11. Make your mind a clean slate.

When you are observing other cultures, do so from a learning and objective mindset. If you find yourself being judgmental, do a thought intervention. Reframe your inner conversation by thinking, "That's interesting. I want to know more." This also means being extra conscious of your own biases, and the need to make people who do things differently wrong.

12. Use the power of hello. Smile and say hello to people in your workplace whether or not they are on your team or look like you.

Workplaces feel more inclusive when people greet each other. It creates a stronger sense of connection.

All too frequently employees feel that they work in places where people don't speak and where the manager just walks by them. They state that they feel invisible.

Saying hello takes no time, costs no money, and can have dramatic results on morale. When hello goes viral, people will be more comfortable asking for and receiving support.

13.   Be aware of the specific international cultures of both the people you work with and your external customers.

If they are bilingual, learn how to say Hello, and Thank-you in their primary language. Your customers and coworkers will feel more comfortable and welcome in your business. This creates memorable customer service experiences, loyalty, return business, and referrals.

14.   Make a greeting self-assessment. Notice the people that you greet most often. Do you tend to look at people and be friendlier with people more like you? If so, start paying attention to people who are not like you.

15.   Be aware of the differences amongst people within other cultures and how those cultures within cultures intersect, i.e. by generation, geography, religion, sexual orientation, etc.

People sometimes think that because they learn about a specific culture that everyone in that culture will be the same.

16. Avoid diversity clichés, like, "I treat everybody the same."

Many managers say they treat everybody the same, and it has become a slogan. Next time your brain prompts you to use that phrase, think about what that really means.

If you treated everyone the same, then everyone would get the same pay, rewards, and feedback. If you treated everyone the same, you wouldn't know how to seek and leverage the diverse talents, skills, and experiences of people in your workplace.

Would you send people in sales and marketing to work in research and development if they didn't have the skills?

Do you give everyone recognition in the same way?

17. Take diversity to lunch.

Invite one person a week who is different than you to lunch. Be curious, and get their perspectives on various work issues. You can talk about how you both came to work at the organization, and what keeps you there. Get to know them as people. Be interested in the differences while looking for commonality.

You may be surprised to find new connections that you never thought would exist.

18.   Use Laser Listening, and be totally focused on the other person you are speaking to. Don't listen with one ear and plan your day with the other. If you tune out you may miss important information. Remember that you have to go beyond your own perspective. If you want people to feel heard, don't trivialize or minimize their concerns or the level of importance they place on an issue.

There are times when you're on a deadline and don't have the time to listen, or you're preoccupied and can't give another person your full attention. It's better to let him or her know this is not a good time than to pretend you're paying attention.

19.   Attend diversity and inclusion programs in your organization whether or not they are mandatory. The more opportunities you have to interact with people who are different than you, the more you'll know and be able to articulate about diversity.

When you do attend a program, think about how to apply what you learned at work and at home.

20.   Attend diversity and inclusion programs outside of work. Share what you learned with people in your organization, and any practical tips that would advance your internal diversity and inclusion processes.

21.   Participate in different employee resource group meetings and events. Give yourself time to become comfortable in places that may be initially

uncomfortable. Get comfortable by talking to one person at a time.

If your organization does not have employee resource groups, there may be other demographically related groups.

22. Take a cross-functional break. Talk to people from other work functions and departments. Find out what they do beyond their title.

A great many people get stuck in silo thinking because they only see the organization from their own work function or department. They don't fully understand the value of other departments and functions. That lack of understanding can cause cross-functional conflict.

23. If you are a member of an Employee Resource Group, or any similar group, personally invite outside people to your meetings or events.

People are more likely to attend when they are invited by another person as opposed to receiving a group email invite.

If possible, tell them what to expect at the meeting and introduce them to other members. This will help them be more comfortable interacting with people in the ERG.

24. If an employee comes out to you as lesbian, bisexual, gay, or transgender, ask how you can be supportive. Some people may not want others to know until they are ready, and other people may want your help sharing the information with employees.

Keep confidentiality. If someone discloses their gender identification or sexual orientation, it's because they trust you and consider you an ally.

25. Educate yourself about LGBT stereotypes

Don't assume that being LGBT means a person has a "different lifestyle." Stop yourself and others from using that term. LGBT people come in all colors and ethnic backgrounds, and have families and people they love. They have all kinds of interests, recreational activities, and lifestyles.

26. Personally extend inclusion

If you attend an event with people you know, welcome and approach people who are alone and may not know anyone. Be available to answer any questions about the group and make an effort to introduce them to other people. You may discover a new volunteer or someone who can add value in some way.

27. Be a diversity and inclusion ambassador.

When a new person joins your team or your department, make a point to welcome him or her. Remember what you wish you had known when you were first hired, and offer any information that could help in the new person's success and cultural acclimation.

The faster they get up to speed, the sooner they can be a productive, contributing member of your team, work group, or organization, and even make your work easier.

28. Attend multicultural events in the community like cultural festivals, ethnic dance performances, and art shows. Bring a friend or colleague and discuss what you saw and what you learned over coffee.

29. Listen to music from different cultures as well as different generations. Research the musical genre, its overall history, and specific songs so you know the meaning and can share your knowledge. Learn about the different styles of music in different cultures.

Ex. People in Mexico listen to different styles of music like Mariachi, Banda, rap and hip-hop, Conjunto, electronic, and salsa depending on age, geography, and personal taste.

30. Research disability and accessibility issues in your workplace and community. Become knowledgeable about different kinds of abilities and disabilities

Identify ways in which you can include people with disabilities. Often people with disabilities feel invisible and are left out of discussions and informal networking.

31. Attend a conference on disability issues, a workshop at a conference, or, if one exists in your organization, a disability related ERG.

Read about the history and movement for disability inclusion in the workplace. Speak up when you hear someone make a disparaging remark about someone with a disability.

32. Take a class in American Sign Language (ASL). Look in the class catalogues at your local community college or adult education program.

33. Research how specific groups are stereotyped. Learn which terms are offensive and which are inclusive for groups relating to race, religion, ethnicity, gender, sexual orientation, etc. Recognize when you hear people use stereotypes when talking about different groups.

34. When you hear a racist or homophobic comment, or a joke that makes fun of, stereotypes, or belittles any group, take responsibility to intervene and stop it. Being silent implies your consent. Be a vocal ally for other groups and ask others to do the same.

35. Respect everyone's gender self-identity and refer to everyone with the name and pronoun they prefer. If you don't know, ask politely. Let them know you are not trying to offend, but want to show respect.

36. Read up on definitions of harassment, hostile work environment, and bullying so you can recognize it and educate others to stop it from happening.

37. Attend and support LGBT community events.

Often people break past their biases by having direct, positive contact with people who are different than them.

38. Teach other people what terms are inclusive and what terms are offensive in regard to ethnicity, race, religion, etc.

39. Learn about other holidays and the different ways people celebrate them.

40. Carve out some time to watch a TV special on other celebrations, do a Google search on a holiday, or check out books at your local bookstore while gift shopping.

41. Learn and practice greetings for different holidays. You'll make people feel appreciated and cared about. This is one of those seemingly small actions that can make a big difference with fellow employees and customers.

42. Try some of the food that people associate with their holidays. While people may celebrate the same holiday, they may not celebrate the same way.

People in Spain observing the same holiday as someone in Russia may not have the same food at their holiday dinner table. Ask questions about the meaning of what you're eating. It's a great way to start a conversation, learn new information, and can be the basis for new relationships.

43. Respect the fact that there are people who do not celebrate any holidays, and don't lecture them if they don't. Everyone makes a choice. Find out what type of events they do celebrate.

44. Read a book about a culture or life different than yours. This can be a biography, autobiography, history book, or tour book.

45. Read a mystery or book of fiction from another culture. You may be surprised at how much you learn about other cultures when you read an engrossing book of fiction.

46. Listen to lectures by people from different cultures and backgrounds. Use print and online sources to learn when and where those lectures will be held. Check out places like The Commonwealth Club, or cultural centers in your area.

47. Make a list of the people you interact with the most. Determine whether they are all the same as you, i.e. - age, culture, race, spiritual or religious practice, sexual orientation, etc. Be conscious of how much diversity is in your life and decide to be curious and interact more with other kinds of people.

48. Attend a religious or spiritual service different than your own. Educate yourself in advance so you can participate with knowledge.

49. Volunteer and participate in multicultural celebrations (Juneteenth, Diwali, Hanukkah, Cinco de Mayo, etc.), or attend a religious service or event different from yours.

50. Join or start a diversity book or film club so you can get other people's perspectives on a book or film.

51. When speaking with people from other cultures, be aware of the idioms you use. While someone may speak excellent English, the idioms you are familiar with may totally confuse him or her.

52. Read, listen, and do your research before you take a stand on issues or current events related to diversity or people different than you. Make sure you have all the facts, and don't jump to conclusions based on race, gender, and ethnicity. Allow yourself to be open to new information, and even a change in outlook.

53. Suggest art, photography, or displays which represent diversity for your lobby and other areas of your office building.

Every supervisor, manager, and leader is responsible for creating, communicating, and promoting the organization's values and culture. The following tips and insights are for anyone who leads others. These tips will help you engage individuals and teams in your mission to leverage diversity and create an inclusive work culture.

23 Simma Lieberman | Copyright 2014 © ALL RIGHTS RESERVED

54. Create a way for employees to offer suggestions, observations, or solve problems for functions or departments other than their own. You might be surprised at the observations people in production have, as well as creative ways to get more done or improve a process.

55. Work in rounds. Organize and lead round table discussions on diversity and inclusion-related issues with people from different levels and functions. Areas for discussion can be on hiring, promotion, information sharing, new hire orientation, or recognition.

56. Ask employees on your team for feedback on how the organization or your department can be more inclusive and take action on doable ideas.

57. Consider informal networking situations. If someone can't meet after work because they have an important obligation, have someone brief them on any important issues discussed or decisions made.

58. Look behind the obvious.

Examine past hiring and promotion patterns. Don't keep only promoting and/or acknowledging the same people or kinds of people repeatedly. Look for people who don't fit a narrow profile.

-Talk to quiet people - you may discover hidden genius.

59. Ask employees at different levels to recommend their peers for new responsibilities, recognition for excellent results, and/or possible promotions. You may be very surprised at the hidden jewels who work in your organization that you are not aware of.

60. Develop a new kind of orientation process.

Create a welcoming process to help new employees learn about the organization, and speed up integration into the company or department. Share your mission and values of diversity management and inclusion so they can get on board.

61. Access diversity of thought. Use different methods to access diversity of thought in meetings, to solve problems, or when you are seeking new ideas. Here are some methods that have been used successfully:

    − Brainstorming - note that brainstorming and speaking out at meetings is one way to solicit ideas, but is not best for everyone. Some people are introverted, so they want to spend more time thinking and share ideas individually.

    − People who don't speak English as their first language may not be comfortable speaking out in a group, and would be more comfortable giving written input.

    − Still others may best generate ideas and solutions working in small groups.

62. Get to know as many of your employees as possible even if they work remotely. Learn the names of three new people in your organization every day, and request that other managers do the same.

63. If someone has a name that is hard to pronounce, ask for the correct pronunciation and write it phonetically.

64. After writing a job description for a new position, review your list of requirements. Determine whether those "requirements" are necessary to the job, personal preferences, or simply "the way we've always done it."

> **Ex.** Just because the last three people who held that position were from Stanford doesn't mean the next person has to have graduated from Stanford.

Does someone really need three years and one month of experience, an ivy league education, or 4.0 GPA to do the job? These factors don't impact how well someone can do the job. Remove these "requirements" from your list.

Determine what competencies and experiences really are necessary, and remove those that are not.

65. List people you have been most comfortable working with in the past. Are they primarily like you? If they

are, then intentionally include people in the candidate pool who seem qualified but are different than you.

Remind yourself that being comfortable with someone doesn't mean they are qualified.

66. When you interview candidates, be conscious of biases and assumptions that could make you negate the candidate's ability without any evidence (too old, too young, "wrong culture").

67. Make hiring decisions on more than just communication style assessments.

Look at the whole person, and know that talent exists beyond where someone falls on a quadrant. They may present one way on an assessment but be better developed in other areas not shown. Use assessments as just one piece of the process.

68. Reserve money in your budget to take new hires to lunch and orient them to the organization, make them feel welcome, and reduce ramp-up time. When people are comfortable with their managers, they are more willing to ask for help to do a better job and prevent or fix costly mistakes.

The faster someone learns the norms and culture of the organization, the more productive they can be in a shorter amount of time.

69. Appoint experienced employees to be "new hire ambassadors." Train them in the right way to welcome new hires.

70. Research and develop a list of colleges that historically have large numbers of women, people with disabilities, and people from different cultural, ethnic, and racial backgrounds. Send recruiting teams to those schools, as well as the "top universities," you may have used in the past.

You want to increase and widen the candidate pool, and expand your options for finding creative people.

71. Provide communication skills and cultural intelligence training for recruiters so they can interact with people from diverse backgrounds at colleges and job fairs. They'll be better able to meet more people and instill interest in your organization amongst potential candidates.

Train recruiters to interview people who look different from them, who don't buy their suits at the same place. Insist they recruit employees who can bring diversity of thought and innovation to your business.

Ex. A CEO of a facilities management company wanted to hire more female managers. Instead of recruiting from his industry, he started attending meetings of women in real estate. "I wanted to find women who would bring different experiences so we could get fresh ideas. I looked for women who understood property management from the client's perspective, and would challenge the way we've always worked. We now have several women in decision-making positions as a result, and we've been able to better serve our clients."

72.   Conduct hiring interviews with a diverse panel. You'll get a wider perspective and be able to assess how well the candidate communicates with people from diverse backgrounds.

73.   Focus on building employee's strengths as opposed to constantly pointing out weaknesses.

Example: A coach was hired to work with a manager who constantly yelled at her employees, belittled them, and criticized them in front of other people. Productivity was suffering, and people were leaving.

Unfortunately, this woman was beyond coaching. She was sure that she was right; that she needed to "set her employees straight," and that they were all trying to "take advantage of the system." She didn't think their quitting was a problem, since "there were others out there waiting to take their jobs."

The company had no choice but to let her go, so that her employees could flourish under a new manager who listened.

74. Recruit early, from middle and high schools. Attend career days and come prepared to discuss the benefits of working for your organization and your industry. Talk to teachers and other students to find out if someone has an interest in a subject related to your industry.

> **Ex.** A manager went to a high school and met a student who didn't have the highest grades, and who at first glance didn't appear to be a potential candidate for his organization. However, in talking to one of the science teachers he discovered that the young man was brilliant in physics and math. The manager jokingly said, "I think I may have found our next Nobel Prize winner." He was so impressed with the young man that he established a mentoring relationship with him, invited him to be an intern when he gets to college, and of course ultimately hopes to hire him.

75. Post links to photos and articles about your company, the importance of diversity within it, and your inclusive culture on Twitter, Facebook, LinkedIn, etc.

76. Build long-term relationships with diversity-related campus organizations, such as those representing Black, Native American, Asian American, and LGBT students, and co-sponsor events with them.

77. Ask leaders of those organizations to suggest and introduce you to potential candidates, and to include notices about your organization in their newsletters. You might be able to submit an article that includes information about diversity and inclusion in your organization.

78. Invite people to switch jobs for a day, or even a few hours.

This will help people work together better, and help prevent misunderstandings about the value of roles and job functions. It's easier to create an inclusive work culture when everyone is part of the big picture.

79. Review all systems and processes (hiring, promotion, evaluations) to determine how inclusive they are. Identify areas for improvement, and work on the one that's easiest to strengthen.

Notify your employees of the plan for changes and keep them apprised of progress.

80. Discuss your diversity values and what inclusion looks like in your organization with contractors, whose behavior can negatively affect your reputation.

This includes security guards, temporary employees, contract call centers, and outside distributors of your products. Educate vendors, contractors, security, etc. about company culture and inclusive behavior. .

A security guard at the SF Contemporary Jewish Museum told two women attending a special Gertrude Stein exhibit that they couldn't hold hands in the museum. When the Executive Director was informed of the situation, she apologized to the women, relieved the security guard of his position, and took full responsibility. The security company was a contractor, not a direct employee of the museum, but the Executive Director didn't make excuses. The security company was made aware of the values and inclusive culture of the museum. Anyone who did not share those values would not be in any official capacity at the museum.

People who represent your organization must model inclusive behavior, even if they're not employees.

81. Establish a formal mentoring program and make it available to all employees. Create a basic structure for mentors and mentees.

82. Identify ways in which your organization is green and involve employees in "green campaigns." It can be as simple as recycling, eliminating waste, or saving electricity. Announce a competition and award a prize

to the group that comes up with the most creative process for sustainability in any aspect of your organization.

83. Consistently make the business case for diversity and inclusion at meetings and events.

People at every level need to understand how they personally benefit from diversity, and be able to articulate what that means in practice with each other and with your customers.

84. Help people understand what other departments do and why they are important to the organization. Too often employees make assumptions about the roles and responsibilities of others, as well as the value other departments bring to the organization. This can create obstacles to sharing resources and information.

85. Create paid internship programs – Add community colleges to your outreach. Widen your net to attract different kinds of people. Use creative marketing to attract people from a diversity of populations.

86. Offer flexible work options such as telecommuting and work at home options when appropriate.

87. If possible give people a choice to restructure their work schedules, such as moving from eight hours five days a week to ten hours four days a week, or more choices for early or late hours.

88. Ask people at every level to articulate how their job contributes to organizational success. You'll find that many people see their work in isolation. Once they understand the value they bring, they are likely to be more motivated, offer suggestions, and be more innovative.

89. Provide constant training and opportunities for continuous learning that are open to everyone, including the person cleaning the floors or answering the phones. People at the lower levels represent your organization. Don't neglect their education.

90. Bring in a facilitator to conduct confidential demographic focus groups so you can get objective feedback about perceived diversity and inclusion strengths, areas needing improvement, and recommendations for change.

91. Develop and support programs and policies that promote life/work balance, and personally model behaviors of self-care and stress management.

92. Ask employees what types of projects or responsibilities they would find challenging. You'll hear new ideas and discover strengths you didn't know existed in your organization.

93. Set up a talent bank where employees can share any of their untapped talents and experience. Before you spend time and money hiring someone from the

outside, check the talent bank. You may find someone who would love to share what they know.

Engage millennials and ask for input instead of managing from a hierarchical, top-down style. Bring older and younger employees together so they can cross-mentor each other.

94. Institute the practice of providing frequent and honest feedback to employees, rather than waiting for the formal evaluation process. Let people have the opportunity to strengthen themselves right away as opposed to six months in the future when it may be too late.

Younger employees in particular want to get feedback as frequently as possible.

95. Spend time getting to know and listening to hourly employees during breaks, in the cafeteria, and at company events. Don't stay in a "management silo."

96. When giving feedback or evaluations, focus on building employee's strengths as opposed to constantly pointing out weaknesses. Provide feedback in private. Never belittle or criticize an employee in front of others.

97. Set up an online and CD library for employees to learn other languages. Reward employees who improve their knowledge of a new language. Make this available to everyone.

98. Enlist your whole leadership team, and identify your fellow champions by the passion they display either in words or actions. Allow them to add to the vision.

Ask your team these questions:

What would make this the kind of workplace that made you jump out of bed every day, even faster than you do now?

If you were one of your direct reports, or an hourly employee, what would need to change to make you want to jump out of bed every day?

What stops this from happening now?

99. Appreciate different styles of leadership.

There are many examples of organizations where talented women were continuously bypassed for promotion, and consequently left to join competitors who recognized their value.

When the CEO of an organization was asked why he never promoted these women, he said, "Those women just weren't strategic enough; I need to find better ones." It took him a while to understand that everyone does not need to be his thought clone and that there were different ways to be strategic and increase profit.

He changed his perspective after the exit of several of the best women in the organization. He became an inclusionist leader, and before he left the organization there were many more women in both senior management and on the executive team.

100. Allow employees to share the meaning of their religious holidays. Understanding other religions and cultures is imperative for cultural intelligence. However, unless you are a religious organization, appearing to endorse one religious belief over another can alienate those that don't share your religious beliefs, and impact their productivity.

101. Find and celebrate events within your organization. Gather a diverse team to organize a year-end, fiscal year end, or spring celebration that leverages the diversity of the team and organization. The team and their work together can serve as a role model for future projects.

102. Create an information process that gives everyone easy access to open positions and promotions. Make sure to include people who work outside of the main headquarters. Let everyone know how he or she can access the information.

103. When people in your organization are not chosen for jobs they've applied for, let them know what they need to work on so they have a better chance next time.

104. Give constructive feedback in private, and develop an improvement plan with input from the employee. Often people will say they understand because they are embarrassed to admit they don't know how to improve or change a behavior.

Notice whether you are giving more feedback to people who look like you than to people who don't. Often managers are uncomfortable giving feedback to people from different cultures, which means that people from different cultures don't know what they are doing well and what needs improvement.

Without feedback it's more likely that people will fail. Give objective, frequent feedback to everyone.

105. Make a list of acronyms commonly used in your organization, and pass them out to new employees (some of the old employees may not know them either).

106. Get to know and develop relationships with people who work in the Diversity and Inclusion department. Share information about their activities with your employees so the Diversity and Inclusion department is integrated within the whole organization, and not just viewed as a separate group or program.

107. Hold a contest where people form diverse teams to develop innovative and doable ideas for new products or services that leverage diversity and increase profit, productivity, or excellent customer experience.

108. Attend Employee Resource or advocacy group cultural events or meetings. You'll be setting the example which will encourage other employees to attend.

- -

109. Have one-on-one conversations with Employee Resource Group leaders, and ask how you can support them.

110. Share your commitments and actions with other managers so they can be similarly engaged.

About Simma Lieberman

Simma Lieberman is internationally known as "The Inclusionist" because she creates inclusive cultures where people love to do their best work, and customers love to do business.

Simma was raised in the Bronx, New York where she developed a passion for diversity and inclusion. She moved to Eugene, Oregon which was her first culture shock, and now lives in the San Francisco Bay Area.

Her clients have included; Gulfstream, Chevron, Kaiser Permanente, Diageo, Oracle, Kimpton Hotel Group, PepsiCo, McDonalds and Genentech as well as numerous public agencies, non-profits and professional associations.

Her articles and advice have been featured in The Wall Street Journal, New York Times, Forbes, Fast Company, CNN, Black MBA, Managing Diversity Journal, and Human Resource Executive. Simma is co-author of *Putting Diversity to Work, How To Successfully Lead a Diverse Workforce, and The Diversity Calling, Building Community One Story At A Time.*

For more information about Simma, please visit www.SimmaLieberman.com, or contact her at Simma@SimmaLieberman.com

59322148R00024

Made in the USA
Lexington, KY
31 December 2016